The Life and Times of Frederick Charles Hobbs

Seafarer & Lifeboat Coxswain

by

Richard E Le Bargy

ISBN: 9798720534394

PublishNation
www.publishnation.co.uk

Introduction

There will be many people like myself who grew up without the benefit of knowing their grandparents. In my case both of my grandfathers died before I was born. Whilst this is not unusual I have always felt a little sad that I was unfortunate in this regard.

In 1940 they were extremely lucky to survive the bombing of the island by German forces. My paternal grandfather Emile worked for Strangers in the Truchot and minutes before the raid had been delivering an order of jam to the Sark boat at the harbour. My mothers father Fred Hobbs was aboard the lifeboat on his way to Jersey when the Luftwaffe attacked the boat killing his eldest son Harold.

Sadly, though, neither of the men survived the war. Emile suffered from a heart condition and as there was a lack of medicines my grandmother sold all of her jewellery to garner enough money to obtain some on the black market. Unfortunately many of the drugs required were unavailable and he died on 3rd March 1944.

Ten days later Fred Hobbs died as a result of head injuries he sustained following an accident a month previously. The alleged accident occurred when he was ordered by the occupiers to accompany a party of German sailors to Fort Doyle. His death was investigated at the time but because of the situation the outcome has always remained questionable, as on his return home immediately following the incident it was discovered that he had been robbed of a considerable amount of money and a gold ring.

During the 1920's he served as chief mate in the merchant navy delivering coal to ports all over the British Isles. On his return to the island he set up as a Boatman taking charge of yachts for wealthy owners as well as skippering the Sark boat White

I

Heather for Captain Clarke of Breqhou. Following the retirement of John Coombes in 1930 he became Coxswain of the Queen Victoria, Guernseys latest lifeboat. During this time he was involved in the rescue of many people in all sorts of perilous situations both on and off the lifeboat as will become clear.

Richard E Le Bargy

Contents

Maps & Charts

IV

Acknowledgements

Mrs M W Tucker (nee Hobbs)

Mrs D Curr (nee Hobbs)

Mrs J Saddler (nee Hobbs)

Mrs A Scrimshaw

Mr D Kreckeler

Mr Carel Toms

Ralph Durand

Guernsey Evening Press

Guernsey Archives

Queen Victoria Crew List 1931 – 1940

Crew Member	Rank	Living at
Frederick C. Hobbs	Coxswain	Cornet St.
Fred Zabiela	2nd Coxswain	Park Lane
A. Stephens	Mechanic	Colborne Rd.
Kenneth Bell	Asst, Mechanic	
W Gurney	Bowman	High St.
T Le Feuvre	Crewman	South Esp.
F Osborne	Crewman	
R Cole	Crewman	Hauteville
W Hobbs	Crewman	
B Noyon	Crewman	
J Mauger	Crewman	
C Farr	Crewman	
Gerald Dunstan	Mechanic	England
Alec Hobbs	Relief Crew	
Harold Hobbs	Relief Crew	
Fred Zabiela Jr.	Relief Crew	

Note – Gerald Dunstan was the English mechanic who came over with the relief lifeboat Alfred & Clara Heath in 1940.

Map showing the Cotentin Peninsula & the Channel Islands

Map showing the South Coast of England the Channel Islands and North West coast of France

VIII

Chapter 1

William Henry Hobbs

The first member of the Hobbs family to settle in the island was Samuel Hobbs who came from Cornwall around 1860. He came to Guernsey to work in the quarrying industry and brought with him his wife Jane and two children William and Cecelia, both being born in Liskeard less than two years before coming to the island.

On arrival the family lived in Paris St. but by 1871 had moved to the Longstore. Samuel and Jane went on to have another nine children making eleven in total. On leaving school William followed his father into what was at that time a flourishing stone industry. And it was whilst working in Alderney as a stonebreaker he met his future wife Mary Jane Henwood. They were married in Guernsey at the Greffe in September 1876. By 1881 William and his wife Mary were living at No22 St Georges Esplanade, the house which adjoins what is now St Georges Hotel. They were also to have eleven children between the years 1879 and 1898. Their fourth eldest, my grandfather, Frederick Charles Hobbs being born in the Pollet in 1885

At some point in the mid 1880's William gave up working in the quarries and became a fisherman. He was associated with the fishing boat Grace Darling and according to his granddaughter Dolly Curr, his wife Mary sold the catch in the Town market. He was a local pilot and also skippered the sailing boat 'Mermaid' which ferried passengers to and from Herm. The 'Mermaid' GU85 was owned by Stanley Mellish who was Herm island manager up until 1914 for the tenant Count Blucher.

Pilot William Henry Hobbs with Boatman aboard
'The Mermaid' off Herm

Picture supplied by Allene Scrimshaw

To highlight the fact that William Henry Hobbs was also heavily involved in locally reported marine incidents there follow two extracts from the 1890's describing typical happenings of that time.

The Comet - Wednesday January 6th 1892
"Last night between the hours of eight and nine, a sailor, one of the crew of the coasting vessel Augia narrowly escaped drowning by falling into the harbour between the three mast brigantine Progress and the quay, having tripped over a fastening. But few individuals were about at the time, and had not his cries for assistance reached Pilot William Hobbs he would certainly have lost his life, there being no object protruding to which he might have clung. Fortunately for the man in peril, Mr Hobbs found a ladder on the deck of the Progress, he, assisted by Mr Spiller, holding it perpendicularly, and thus enabling the sailor to ascend to safety after reaching its friendly aid".

The Comet - Wednesday July 6th 1892
"While cruising some three miles off Sark on Monday in the pilot boat Flying Foam, Messrs Henry Horsham and W H Hobbs fell in with a partly submerged puncheon, which they took in tow and brought to the harbour of St Peter Port, occupying 12 hours in the transit. On being examined by the States guager it was found to contain 137 gallons of Claret - We learn that other flotage in the form of casks of claret has been picked up".

William also served on the pulling and sail lifeboats, probably the Vincent Wilkinson Kirk Ella and Arthur Lionel in the 1890's and early 1900's. It was indeed natural therefore that his two sons William and Frederick would both pursue a career at sea and furthermore follow their fathers lead by continuing the Hobbs tradition aboard the lifeboat which was to last for over fifty years. William Henry Hobbs died on 25th May 1923 at his home 17 Cornet St aged 72 (*his age was more like 64)* and buried at Candie Cemetery on Monday 28th May 1923. An obituary which appeared in the Guernsey Weekly Press of June 2nd 1923 page5 stated the following:-

DEATH OF AGED LIFEBOATMAN
"The death occurred on Friday May 25th of Mr W Hobbs, aged 72 years. A lifeboatman who had taken part in many adventures of the sea and as reliefs in Victorian days. Mr Hobbs resided at

17 Cornet Street. Following the sea on Foreign and Home trade since a lad. He was ill but a week and leaves a widow, two sons and four daughters. Sons Mr William and Fred Hobbs."

Both Hobbs brothers served in the Merchant Navy and later skippered sailing and motor yachts for wealthy local owners. During the 1st World War William the eldest, was torpedoed by a German U-boat whilst aboard the SS Longbenton. Surviving this action he went on after the war to take charge of a number of small vessels berthed at St Peter Port, and was a well-known character at the harbour. Likewise his brother Fred also served on merchant shipping attaining the rank of Chief Officer.

In 1907 Frederick Hobbs married Reta Maud Brehaut at the Greffe. They also had eleven children the eighth eldest being my mother Merlin Winifred Hobbs born in September 1924. When I decided to compile this brief history I was fortunate that both my mother and her elder sister Dolly Curr were so keen to support the project, for without their valuable input and recollections the task would have been extremely difficult. For example my mother had spent many hours as a young girl helping her father to write up his logs which recorded cargoes together with their points of departure and landing. My Aunt Dolly was also able to lend me postcards sent home by my Grandpa between 1909 and 1920. The cards were very informative and showed that Grandpa was a very caring family man despite the fact that he spent so much time at sea. For most of these years he was serving aboard merchant transports carrying coal from the north-east coasts of England and Scotland down to London and as far as Galway in Ireland, one of the colliers he sailed aboard being the HMT Southwark. Following the end of the First World War he was awarded the Mercantile Marine War Medal.

The Hobbs Family circa 1918

Fred & Reta Hobbs and their four eldest
L-R Ruth, Olive, Doris (Dolly) & Harold

Chapter 2

The Mermaid

This story begins on Sunday 28th December 1919 and ends in the first week of the new decade 1920. As it unfolds it becomes clear that if a difficult job was to be undertaken there was no better man than Fred Hobbs at the tiller. His considerable knowledge of local waters must have been well known by those involved with pilotage and the like. For it was to him they turned when the unexpected happened.

Mr Stanley Mellish the owner of the Mermaid was requested to take a passenger to Jersey, the usual skipper William Hobbs being unavailable Mr Mellish approached Williams's son Fred Hobbs and Pilot John Gillman to serve as crew. The following report entitled "Three Men in a Boat" appeared in the Guernsey Evening Press of 3rd January 1920.

"One of the most thrilling triumphs over wind and wave was the story which the hardy crew of three on the good and stout fishing boat Mermaid had to tell when they put into St Peter Port at 8.30 last night after a 34 hour battle in stormy seas.

The Mermaid left Guernsey at 11 o'clock on Sunday morning for Jersey, taking across a passenger who had missed the mail boat, said Skipper Gillman to one of our representatives this morning. On board were Mr Stanley R Mellish, Pilot John Gillman of La Tourgand and Mr Fred Hobbs of Lower Hauteville. The weather was fine but a heavy S.S.W. wind was blowing, and the crew were soaked when they arrived at St Helier at 7 o'clock on Sunday night.

The winds remained considerable in force during the week, and it was impossible to leave for Guernsey until Thursday morning, when at 10 o'clock with a north-east wind blowing lightly, it was decided to make for Guernsey. All went well till abreast of the Corbiere, which was reached at 12 o'clock. There then began to be indications of a freshening wind. Suddenly at 1.30 when some seven miles west of the Corbiere, the wind caught the craft with great force, and carried away the mainsail which was lowered. Next the foresail was torn to ribands and this was hauled down.

It was then obvious that the journey onward must be abandoned. A storm jib was rigged up aft to replace the mainsail, and so steady the craft, and this done it was decided to make for St Brelades Bay, which was reached at 5.30. The anchors were dropped within the bay. A considerable sea was running, and the bows were submerging in the rollers. This was a most anxious time for all on board, for apparently the Mermaid was unnoticed from the shore. During the hours till midnight the spare clothing of the men was saturated with paraffin and seven or eight flares were burnt.

During this vigil Pilot Gillman received a severe injury. One of the anchor ropes got out of the score, and in catching the rope to haul it back into position Pilot Gillman's finger got crushed on the rail as the rope suddenly became taut.

Another incident followed at midnight when the ropes parted from the anchors. It was then decided to put the head of the Mermaid to sea, and the head of the foresail was made fast to the head of the gaff. Three reefs were put in and with this Pilot Gillman elected to make for the Roches Douvres, if possible, to avoid going ashore on Les Minquiers. The long night was spent in drifting about, but at any rate the crew had the satisfaction of knowing their bearings and though they were drenched to the skin, and labouring in heavy seas, their position was never in doubt and the doughty Mermaid was maintaining her reputation as the finest little craft known in the Channel Islands.

When daylight broke the wind was north-east, and it was deemed wise to make for France, Paimpol, becoming the new objective. So the journey was commenced to the Roches Douvres. The wind veered to westward when off the Roches Douvres and then the whole enterprise became changed, this time gladly, for the new objective was Guernsey – and home.

Shortly after 4 o'clock a steamer was sighted to the westward and was spoken to by the Mermaid. The steamer was on passage to St Malo, and the captain looking at the hardy crew, offered to tow them to the French port. But with a favourable wind the crew elected to see the thing through, and their requirements – a jar of water – was gladly passed to them from the French steamer. And so the hours sped till Guernsey became more than a blot on the horizon, and in the light of afternoon with a blaze of yellow around it – recalling the angry seas that brought disaster to 'The Skippers Daughter' – so well told by Longfellow – the little Mermaid, with her tattered sails bearing the evidence of rude patching and repair crossed the pierheads and came proudly sailing under the grim shadow of Castle Cornet – a battlement of the wave as the great Castle was of the land.

Today the crew were indulging in a well-earned rest while most of the population were astir, but we were fortunate enough to obtain interviews before going to press. Pilot Gillman's hand and arm are swollen, due to the severe crushing of the finger.

But above all there is evident pride in the heart of the three members of the crew in the manner which the Mermaid outrode the furies of wind and wave: and probably the public will accost some measure of this triumph to the crew, who though drenched to the skin – their clothes dried on them twice – kept their little craft intact, repaired her torn sails, kept her pumps going and so arrived "at the haven where they would be" greatly to the relief of anxious relatives and friends.

Interviewed by a 'Press' representative this morning Mr Stanley Mellish said – "A passenger who had missed the Ibex for Jersey called on me last Sunday and requested me to take him down to Jersey. I told him that if he could get my crew to consent to go I would come and drive the motor. To my surprise he returned and said that they had consented. We left Guernsey about 11am and after a dirty trip arrived in St Helier at 7pm. The rain was so heavy that we could not see the harbour lights, but managed to finally moor the Mermaid safely in harbour and landed at the old Great Western berth.

We were weather bound in Jersey until Thursday morning, when the weather having moderated and a southerly wind prevailing, we decided at 10.45 to make a start for Guernsey. After rounding the Corbiere the wind shifted to the north-west, but we proceeded against the headwind until about 10 miles from the Corbiere lighthouse, when it increased to a gale, and our canvas was practically carried away. We had to about ship and rig up two spare jibs as mainsail foresail and try and make Jersey again. A huge sea – I have never seen the sea get up so quickly before – was running, but we managed to sail past the dreaded Jailers and then endeavoured to make St Brelades Bay.

However the gale was too strong, and under this reduced canvas and the motor we could not make headway towards the shore, and so dropped anchor. This was carried away after about half-an-hour, and the second – the only remaining one – was dropped immediately – half way between Noirmont Point and St Brelades Bay – which held in the rocky bottom. In the meantime, when we dropped the first anchor, flares were sent up, but no reply was forthcoming from shore. Then the punt, which was towing astern by two stout painters, was carried away. The ring-bolt to which one painter was fastened was pulled out, and also the thwart to which the other one was fastened was pulled clean out of the punt.

Shortly after this the second anchor parted, and we hoisted small canvass in the hope that by beating about offside the Corbiere until daylight we might be seen by either the Alberta from Guernsey or the Ibex from Jersey. The gale, however, had by daylight taken us a long way to sea in the direction of the Roches Douvres

As the morning advanced the wind moderated and the smoke of a steamer making her way in the direction of St Malo was seen. On observing our signals of distress – I used my old engine

9

jumper and a small red flag as signals – the steamer changed her course and bore down towards us. The wind mean while had changed to the southward, and we decided to make for Guernsey, and only asked the Captain of the steamer to refill our water jar which had rolled over and emptied itself some hours previously. This the captain readily did for us, and also most kindly offered to tow us as far as St Malo, telling us that in his opinion, there was a strong blow coming from the southward. He also promised to wire from St Malo to the Harbourmaster, Guernsey, that we were on our way to that port under greatly reduced canvas.

The wind rapidly increased, and under sail and motor we made splendid headway, and about 6pm sighted the Hanois Light. With wind and tide and motor we were making good progress, with heavy following seas – which lifted the Mermaid and slung her forward without putting any water aboard, and finally St Martins Point was passed and we felt that our troubles were nearly over.

The Mermaid

Under a very small mainsail and the motor still ticking well, we rounded the pierheads and safely moored the Mermaid at about 8pm. A ketch anchored close by was hailed and kindly put us ashore in their boat, enquiring from us on the way: "Are you the chaps that are supposed to be drownded? Is your boat the Mermaid, because if so we've been hearing ashore that you're lost." Climbing up the ladder at the end of the Victoria arm, we put foot on old Guernsey at last, and immediately shook hands with each other: then hastening off to our homes to be received with tremendous enthusiasm and thankfulness.

I should like to say that my two mates, John Gillman and Fred Hobbs the son of the usual skipper of the Mermaid, behaved most splendidly. Fred Hobbs taking the tiller the whole time with the exception of the Thursday night, when he was taken really ill with a severe attack of ague. Gillman then stepping into the breach and taking the whole night watch himself. It would be impossible to have two more stout hearted men with one in such a dreadful time."

Chapter 3

The Merlin

It is known that at least two of his children were named after boats that he had been associated with. My aunt Pat who had always thought she had been christened Evelyn Patricia was shocked when she learned that her birth had been registered at the Greffe as Evelyn Pattie. It turned out that he had been aboard a boat called Pattie on or around the time of her birth!

The same rule was also applied to my mother who was named after Colonel Elliot's fine yacht the Merlin. In 1923 Colonel Elliot who was managing director of Bucktrouts commissioned Fred to go and collect the newly built Merlin from Swanage and return her to Guernsey. The appearance of this boat must have been considered quite newsworthy as a report describing her arrival in the harbour was printed in the Guernsey Weekly Press of 26th May.

The Arrival of the Merlin

"Beautiful in a freeboard suit of white, and of very comfortable appointments, Col A.L.Elliotts fine motor auxiliary yacht Merlin arrived in the Pool yesterday after an 18 hours run from Swanage, which she left at noon on Thursday, in charge of Mr F Hobbs with J Wheadon on board.

The Merlin was designed by Harley Mead and was built at Falmouth. Her 7 h.p. Parsons engine drives her at five knots. Of 31ft length overall, 10ft beam and 6ft draught she is 11 tons, and her handsome cabin is ideal for accommodating parties on pleasure trips among any of the islands of the archipelago. The Merlin is a handsome addition to island craft and certainly is lending a touch of beauty to the Pool."

My mother Merlin Winifred Hobbs was born fifteen months later on 10th September 1924.

It has been established that he brought the Merlin into St Peter Port on the same day that his father William Hobbs died. It is not known however whether or not he was able to see his father before he passed away.

The Merlin in the Pool 1928

Chapter 4

The Echo

As mentioned earlier Fred was a respected boatman in local waters and was employed by many wealthy clients, none more so than Mr E Phillips Oppenheim who came to the island from America in 1934. An author of several internationally renowned espionage and thriller books Mr Edward Phillips Oppenheim b. London 1866 lived in a large house in Le Vauquidor. After leaving school at 17 Oppenheim had worked in his fathers leather business and began writing in his spare time. His first novel 'Expiation' in 1886 was read by a New York businessman who bought out the leather business thus making Mr Oppenheim a very rich man. Among his better known works are 'The Moving Finger' (1911) and 'The Great Impersonation' (1920) which was eventually made into a film. He was a very popular man in island circles and was known affectionately as 'Oppy'

The Echo was a fine motor yacht and always stood out at local regattas and as Fred was her skipper a close liaison with Mr Oppenheim was forged. In the 1920s the Echo won a prestigious class at the Cowes Regatta which delighted both owner and skipper alike.

There follows some extracts from Mr Oppenheims biography 'Pool of Memory' published 1942 in which he makes mention of the Echo.

"The small yacht on which we spent such pleasant times in Garoupe I sold soon after leaving the South of France. I parted from her with deep regret, but her draught made her an impossible proposition. She was too small to face the Bay of Biscay and the sea voyage home; on the other hand, she drew too much water for the canals. We compromised by re-christening the motor yacht I bought in Southampton the 'Echo'

and although she never took quite the same place in our affections, she was considerably larger and her accommodation was much more adequate. We spent several very pleasant summers on her."

The Echo in 1940
Picture supplied by Joan Saddler nee Hobbs

At the North regatta in August 1937 the Echo was at her startling best, so much so that the Guernsey Press included her in their Weekly Press of 26th August. The picture shows the Echo dressed overall with crew aboard overlooked by Mont Crevelt tower. Inset on the left is the president of the Regatta, Mr E. H. Troutead talking with Mr Phillips Oppenheim, also in shot is Mr Gervase F. Peak's motor yacht 'Rambler'. The article that accompanied the picture reads as follows.

At 3 o'clock Mr E Phillips Oppenheims Echo weighed anchor for a cruise and Mr F Hobbs megaphoned from the bridge "We shall join your party this evening" to which news the Committee saluted the departing novelist and his party.

15

The picture also appears in the Carel Toms book 'Reflections of Guernsey'. Hoping to obtain an image I contacted Mr Toms who was delighted to supply me with the copy seen below.

The Echo
Picture supplied by Mr Carel Toms

A month after the regatta in September 1937 Mr Phillips Oppenheim was cruising the French canals aboard the Echo with Fred Hobbs at the helm. Also on board were his valet, assistant secretary and a crew of five. What started out as a normal late summer vacation turned into a trip that was far from ordinary. The report in the Guernsey Weekly Press of 30th September describes the events in some detail with the headline 'Guernsey Yacht in Two Sea Dramas'. The sub headings went on as follows 'Epic Rescue work by the Echo – Three Lives Saved' and 'The Nimble pounded to pieces in WNW Gale'. The story goes on to report –

Twice during a cruise just completed in the North of France, Mr Phillips Oppenheim the famous author and owner of the yacht Echo, was confronted with situations which are usually associated with the film screen.

The crew of the Echo, captained by Mr Fred Hobbs saved the lives of three gentlemen who were on a twelve day cruising holiday, and it was also through Mr Hobbs that the authorities were acquainted with the true facts regarding the 'Renown' the Brixham yacht that had been reported missing. Over the radio the public had heard of the disappearance of the Renown and how, following a broadcast SOS search was being made for it. Today the Evening Press presents the authentic version of the drama from Mr Hobbs.

In a graphic account of the entry into Havre harbour of the Renown, Mr Hobbs remained reticent and modest regarding the activities of himself and the crew of the Echo in order to render assistance to the Brixham yacht.

The Echo was already anchored in Havre harbour, heavy seas were running and to make conditions worse a gale was blowing when the already sorely buffeted Renown attempted to enter the harbour. Before the Echo's crew could attempt to aid her in any way Renown had suffered severe damage to the starboard side and was in great danger, when reaching the damaged yacht just before the Echo a powerful French tug hailed the Renown and took her in tow safely to the inner yacht basin. The French tug had just forestalled the Echo, for it was Mr Hobbs intention to render assistance in the same way as the tug had done. Mr Hobbs knowing the anxiety and suspense concerning the crew of the Renown immediately informed the authorities, who made it known that the yacht was safe, to the widespread relief of relations and friends.

Saved Three Lives – But the Echo's adventures were not yet finished; even greater thrills were yet to come. In a different setting and under worse conditions the Echo and crew were responsible for saving the lives of three men.

The Echo had put into Deauville for shelter at night. Heavy seas were running and a WNW wind was blowing hard. The cutter yacht 'Nimble', jointly owned by Messrs CA de Cosson and F Kemmis Betty, was following the Echo. The Echo safely gained the shelter of Deauville, but when the 'Nimble', following behind, attempted to make the harbour they were blown right across onto the sands at Deauville, being carried ashore with the raging sea pounding on top of them. As soon as the 'Nimble' had been perceived to miss the entrance action was taken by the Echo's crew, the master and crew of the 'Dellrose' another yacht anchored in Deauville and the assistance of the Deauville lifeboat was called for. Mr Hobbs and the master of the 'Dellrose' offered to man with their crews the lifeboats themselves. Taking the matter into their own hands, the Echo's master decided that something must be done to save the 'Nimble' and her crew, who were already in a perilous position, so the Echo put out of harbour to effect an eleventh hour rescue. Within a quarter of an hour the 'Nimble', now entirely at the mercy of the elements was battered to pieces. To quote Mr Hobbs own words " She opened just like a kipper". The crew of three of the 'Nimble' had put on lifebelts and were already in the water, when the Echo arrived were hauled out and taken aboard the Guernsey yacht.

The three rescued yachtsman were hospitably received by Mr Phillips Oppenheim and were given dry clothes, warm drinks and food and they soon recovered from their adventure. All their belongings were lost with the exception of the Nimbles lifebelts, which were presented by the Nimbles owner to Mr Hobbs in recognition of his gallant services.

Arrangements were then made with a French café for the three rescued yachtsmen's night's lodgings. In the morning they went on to Dieppe, from there back to London. The 'Nimble' was an auxiliary yawl constructed at Dartmouth in 1891, and is attached to the port at Dartmouth. The cruise of the Echo, which was so dramatically interrupted, was one that embraced Cherbourg, Deauville, up the river Seine to Rouen then back through the Havre canals. The cruise was only half completed when the rescues took place. Mr Phillips Oppenheim was aboard the Echo accompanied by his assistant secretary and valet, the boat was manned by a crew of five with Mr Fred Hobbs in command. The Echo is now anchored in the Pool.

So yet another episode in the Echo's varied history comes to a happy conclusion with Grandpa at the forefront of the action.

Oppy liked nothing more than a good days fishing and would muck in just like one of the crew. He also enjoyed entertaining and the extract that follows perfectly highlights the fact that if he could combine the two, then so much the better. In the extract from 'The Pool of Memory' he talks about a trip to Sark where he lunched with the Dame, her husband and General Sir Frederick Maurice of the Sherwood Foresters regiment. Grandpa was at the helm, also aboard was Sark fisherman Lawrence Roberts.

"After lunching on board with the Dame of Sark and her husband on fine lobster. The Dame retired to leave the party to fish. We had no sooner settled down on the Pollack ground than I saw Hobbs and Roberts conferring together, both shading their eyes and pointing to a curious streak in the distance, Mackerel! I exclaimed. Even as I spoke we could see them, little glittering specks of silver jumping a few inches out of the water, up came the anchor and away we went, out came the mackerel lines with the dazzling spinners attached"

Before the outbreak of the Second World War Mr Oppenheim and his family left the island and the Echo was laid up at the careening hard in St Peter Port. Grandpa fearing that the Germans might occupy the island stripped all the valuable fittings from the boat and put them into safe keeping. Unfortunately the beautiful yacht deteriorated during the five years of occupation and was eventually scrapped. The various accessories that had been carefully stowed away were offered back to Mr Oppenheim on his return to the island in 1945 but he generously suggested that they should be sold with the proceeds going to the Hobbs family. Thus the remaining parts of the Echo were disposed of at the auction rooms.

Shortly after his return to the island he loved Mr Oppenheim died at the age of eighty at his residence in Le Vauquidor

CAPT F.C.Hobbs. Phillip. OPPENHEIM. Larry, Roberts.

Laying crabpots near La Gorge Rock, east of Sark
Picture supplied by Joan Saddler nee Hobbs

Chapter 5

The Queen Victoria

The States purchased Guernsey's first lifeboat in 1803 at a cost of £170. She was built in England by Henry Greathead and was based on the design of his first lifeboat the 'Original' in the 1790's.

It would appear that this boat was never used, in fact, for the next 125 years the various lifeboats stationed in the island were only launched a total of 17 times and gave assistance on only two of these occasions. The reasons for the ineffectiveness of these early boats are many, the high rise and fall of tide, the weather and the ill thought locations of their boathouses being some of the major factors. Very often the lifeboat had to be drawn down to the water by horses and launched in the most difficult of circumstances. There are also accounts of it being transported across the island by road which was far from ideal, as by the time it had arrived on the opposite coast invariably the distressed vessel had either sunk or been dealt with by the local fishermen.

At other times it would be towed by steam tug if the casualty was some distance off. Often though the tugs would not wait for the lifeboat and go off in search of the troubled ship alone. Other rescues were effected by the various pilot cutters moored around the coast. On the evening of Thursday 16th January 1851, pilot John Mitchell in his boat 'Queen' rescued three people from the French cutter 'Adele' bound from St Malo to Guernsey. For this act of bravery he was awarded a silver medal from the R.N.L.I.

The only reported incident of the Guernsey lifeboat saving lives during the pulling and sail era was in 1895, when on 14th February the schooner 'Isabella Helen' en route from Plymouth was attempting to enter St Peter Port in a strong easterly gale. Unable to make harbour she was forced to drop anchor near a dangerous outcrop of rock in Havelet bay. In response to her desperate calls for help the lifeboat Vincent Wilkinson Kirk Ella was launched under the charge of Coxswain Frederick Rich, and, with assistance from the tug 'Alert' a line was got aboard 'Isabella Helen', she was then towed to the safety of the harbour.

Incredibly another thirty-five years were to elapse before the States in conjunction with the R.N.L.I. made the decision to station a motorised lifeboat at St Peter Port. This was despite a great deal of public criticism of the service in years past. However things were about to change.

On 27th October 1929 the last of the pulling and sail lifeboats Arthur Lionel was replaced by a Barnett Class boat ON719 built by Samuel Wight at Cowes. Powered by two 60hp Weyburn petrol engines she was capable of a top speed of eight and a half knots. The ON719 later to be renamed the Queen Victoria was of 51ft overall length with a beam of 13ft 6inches. Her first coxswain was John Coombes with 2nd Cox F De Carteret and a further crew of six making eight in total.

The new lifeboat carried out her first rescue on 25th February 1930 towing the States lighter with three men aboard into St Peter Port. The lighter had run into trouble in a strong breeze whilst working on the s.s. Beauport, which had been wrecked on the Agenor rock.

In August 1930 after 14 years as coxswain, John Coombes retired and was succeeded by Frederick Charles Hobbs.

Queen Victoria at St Peter Port 1931

The above photograph recording the naming ceremony carried out by the then Governor Lord Ruthven shows Coxswain Hobbs standing in the bow of the boat (left) with hundreds of islanders and officials looking on from the White Rock pier. The introduction of this modern motorised vessel was hugely successful as she was able to put to sea regardless of weather or sea conditions unlike her predecessors. She was called upon several times in the 1930's saving many lives.

Chapter 6

The Capri

The first significant rescue carried out by the Guernsey lifeboat Queen Victoria under the guidance of Coxswain Frederick Charles Hobbs took place in the early hours of Thursday September 22nd 1932. The Capri a 35-ton ketch rigged yacht had been driven across the channel from the south coast of England by a strong northeasterly gale ending up near Les Hanois lighthouse. The captain of the ill-fated yacht said that he and his party had left Poole with the intention of cruising the south-coast when his boat was overtaken by a strong gale. He hove-to for thirty-seven hours but eventually found himself off the west coast of Guernsey where he took shelter in the lee of Pleinmont cliffs. After going ashore to check the weather situation he was advised by two local fishermen that the yacht should be moved as its present position was felt to be unsafe. Reluctant to do this as one of the engines was suspect, the captain Mr R Christopher re-joined his craft to attempt the manoeuvre.

Shortly after getting under way the yachts engines failed and they were forced to drop anchor much closer to a group of rocks than they would have liked. At this point it was decided that flares should be burnt to summon help. In response to these flares the lifeboat was summoned at 1.20am. The Queen Victoria set course for Les Hanois under Coxswain Hobbs and full crew passing the pierheads fifteen minutes later. The lifeboat made steady headway along the south coast and arrived off Les Hanois at 2.35am.

The coxswain, interviewed later explained the action in his own words. " I was at home at 1 o' clock when I received a telephone message from the exchange that there was a vessel in distress off the Hanois. I dressed and was at the Station within five minutes of the call. My crew collected smartly. At the station were

24

Advocate H H Randell and Mr W Frampton. Mr Randell then informed me that a vessel was showing distress signals about one mile north of the Hanois. We proceeded to sea in the Queen Victoria and passed the pierheads at 1.34am and in one hour reached the vessel. The sea was very rough and it was low water."

He continued "On approaching the yacht we saw flares: the crew were burning a blanket saturated in paraffin. We spoke to the yacht, which had two anchors down. She was in a maze of rocks. The stern anchor was keeping her away from the Round Rock, only a few feet away from her stern. It required careful manoeuvring in the darkness to approach the Capri, for submerged rocks were all around us."

"The owner spoke to me, and I suggested that a tow rope should be taken on board. This we did successfully, the Queen Victoria getting within two yards of the Capri. We then made an attempt to tow her. Unhappily the crew were unable to slip their anchors in time to get away and the tide was veering the Queen Victoria on to a dangerous reef in a wind which was blowing fresh from the east-south-east. There was no help for it, it was necessary to chop away the tow rope to get the lifeboat away from the danger she was in."

"I then took a round turn and made a second attempt at towing, which succeeded. We towed her away from the big rock, and had towed the Capri a short distance when she sheered and struck a submerged rock and started making water rapidly. The crew informed me that there was between four and five feet of water in the cabin, so I requested them to come onto the lifeboat, and came alongside for the purpose. Mr W Gurney the signaller then sent a message by morse to Advocate Randell, with Mr Frampton at Pleinmont Point informing him that the crew were safe and we were returning to St Peter Port"

"So we proceeded back through the Hanois rocks, along the south coast and arrived in harbour at 5.37 this morning"

Coxswain Hobbs went on to say "Had she taken a right sheer we should have got her out the second time" He said that it was unfortunate that the anchors had not been slipped in time at the first attempt.

The Capri, which was registered at Fowey in Cornwall, sank about six minutes after striking the submerged rock. Fortunately the crew of four including the owner had by this time been taken aboard the Queen Victoria. In conclusion the owner Mr R Christopher said that he and his friends greatly admired the splendid way in which the coxswain and crew of the St Peter Port lifeboat had got them away from their precarious situation. The unfortunate loss of the yacht was "just a sheer misfortune". On arrival at St Peter Port the rescued crew were accommodated at the Royal Hotel.

The names of those aboard the lifeboat were Coxswain F Hobbs, Cornet St, Second Cox, Mr F Zabiela, Park Lane. Mr A Stephens, Colborne Rd, Motor Mechanic, Mr Kenneth Bell, Assistant Motor Mechanic, Mr W Gurney, High St, Bowman, Mr T Le Feuvre, South Esplanade, Mr F Osborne, Mr R Cole, Lower Hauteville.

Les Hanois Lighthouse 2007

Picture by Nigel Byron

Chapter 7

The Leander

There were but few times during the 1930's that the Queen Victoria put to sea under the command of anyone other than Fred Hobbs. However it is testament to the skills and abilities of the men of the RNLI that they were able to take control in the absence of their Coxswain. Such a situation occurred on the night of the 16th March 1934 when the lifeboat went in search of a fishing boat under the charge of 2nd Coxswain Fred Zabiela.

Captain James Ingrouille of 22 Les Canichers and Mr William Bichard of Les Hubits, St Martins had set out at 10.15 that morning on an ormering expedition in Mrs W Bichards boat the Leander. They had aboard a young man whom they landed in Herm, after dropping off their passenger they then took the boat around to the back of Herm by which time a strong wind had blown up. Shortly after reaching their destination the boats engine failed due to lack of fuel and the two men resolved to sail the Leander with the tide back toward Fort Doyle on Guernsey's north coast.

However when they reached a point near the Platte Fougere lighthouse they found that the tide was running too strongly to warrant the attempted journey towards the harbour. Meanwhile the man they had dropped off in Herm had returned with Fred Zabiela's trip, and on landing was surprised to learn that nothing had been heard of his companions. The news was passed to Mr Bichards son who sought out Coxswain Hobbs. Together they searched the north-east shoreline by motorcar, investigating, with the aid of a beachlamp, the many craggy inlets along the coast. Mr Hobbs was not unduly concerned, as he anticipated that if in difficulties, a sailor of Captain Ingrouilles experience would seek shelter somewhere in the vicinity of their search.

Eventually they located the boat in the darkness, apparently disabled. Coxswain Hobbs immediately made a telephone call from Fort Doyle to the lifeboat station to ascertain whether a report had been received. He then learned that the lifeboat had already left its station. The Queen Victoria had been summoned by rockets at about 8.20. The crew had waited in vain for about fifteen minutes for their coxswain to appear, but when he made no show she sailed under 2nd Cox F Zabiela, finally leaving port at 8.45 p.m.

She made good headway, arriving at the scene around 9.10 p.m. The men on the fishing boat noticed the approach of the lifeboat and struck lights to give their position. By this time the tide was high with quite a heavy set running. The wind was gusting between 40 and 50 mph causing huge breakers to cascade the surrounding rocks with white foam. The excited onlookers who had gathered in the vicinity of Fort Doyle watched anxiously as the lifeboat negotiated a precarious channel through the maze of rocks with her searchlight scanning the area for signs of the stricken vessel. She was also sending messages by Morse lamp that were being picked up by Mr A Mahy, a former Yeoman of Signals R.N. who had stationed himself on the headland for that purpose.

The Queen Victoria finally came alongside the Leander at about 9.55 p.m despite the heavy gale that was blowing. The gathered crowd were able to hear verbal communication between the two vessels, and shortly before 10 p.m a message was flashed to shore to say that the lifeboat was going to tow the boat back to St Peter Port. She arrived back in harbour at 11.30 p.m. with the Leander and her tiny punt trailing behind and both Captain Ingrouille and Mr Bichard safe below decks of the valiant Queen Victoria.

Chapter 8

Vain Search at Night

As anyone who has been involved with lifeboats will know, there are times when a call-out will result in a fruitless search. Far from being a waste of time, it is by its nature a comfort to all those men of the sea who know that brave lifeboat crews will turn out in all weathers at the slightest hint that someone may be in trouble.

An example of this type of incident happened on the evening of Sunday November 4th 1934. The report of rocket flares being sighted off the south coast of the island led to the lifeboat maroons being fired. This action caused quite a commotion in many churches in the town and it wasn't long before a large crowd had gathered at the harbour to witness the despatch of the Queen Victoria.

The crew under Coxswain Hobbs mustered within 18 minutes and the lifeboat sped out of St Peter Port at 7.35p.m. A confused report first indicated that the vessel in distress was off the Corbiere in Jersey, but it was later confirmed that the probable position was 5 miles south-west of Corbiere in Guernsey. A great number of people had collected at vantage points on the headlands at Icart and Jerbourg in an attempt to track the progress of the Queen Victoria which had made good headway and by 8.15 p.m. was five miles southwest of St Martins point.

A Mr Gerald Lewis of Vaux Huberts, St Martins, who said that he had seen what was thought to be rockets out at sea, had first raised the alarm. Estimating that they were being fired at around seven or eight a minute, he immediately contacted Mr W Frampton, Secretary of the local RNLI which resulted in the lifeboat being summoned at 7.22p.m.

Shortly after the lifeboat had left her mooring, Mr Frampton, Captain Penstone Franklin (Harbourmaster), Mr H E Marquand (States Supervisor) and Mr H H Randell (Chairman of the local RNLI) departed by car for Icart Point. Nothing could be seen from there and consequently the Queen Victoria was recalled.

When the lifeboat returned to St Peter Port harbour at 9.40p.m., Coxswain Hobbs related that he had steered a course to a point seven miles S.S.W. of St Martins Point, but saw no vessel in distress. A small fishing boat was discovered fishing S.S.E. of the Gaudains and he was of the opinion that the lights may have originated from her. Some uncertainty remained with regards to a phone call received that evening from Jersey. It would appear that a Mr Rivers phoned Mrs Hobbs the Coxswains wife to say that he had received a message from Guernsey saying that there was a vessel in distress off the south-east coast of the island, but there were no signs of a ship. Visibility was perfect and Coxswain Hobbs reported a very calm sea

Apart from the Coxswain, those on board the Queen Victoria were – 2nd Cox F Zabiela, Messrs W Gurney, W Hobbs, R Cole, T Le Feuvre, A Stephens and B Noyon.

Chapter 9

The Frolic

On the afternoon of 16th November 1934, two fishermen who had been lifting their crab-pots off the south coast found themselves in difficulties when the engine of their motor boat failed to restart.

Fortunately their plight had been spotted from the shore as they drifted helplessly, and as a consequence the lifeboat was launched. After a long search the craft was located and towed back to the harbour by the Queen Victoria.

The alarm had been raised shortly before 6 p.m. by Mr P J Dorey of the Gouffre Hotel and by Mr J F Merrien of Les Villets, Forest. They reported that a small boat had been seen drifting towards the Corbiere and those aboard could be heard blowing their hooter.

At 5.55 p.m. the lifeboat was called out by Mr H H Randell. The crew put in a remarkably fast turn out and shortly after the signal maroons had been fired the Queen Victoria slipped her moorings and was underway in the charge of Coxswain Hobbs. Mr Randell and Mr W Frampton, Secretary of the local RNLI immediately went by motor car to the south coast where they took up a position high above the Pleinmont cliffs. A small crowd had gathered on the clear moonlit night to witness the proceedings. But after a telephone call was made to the Gouffre Hotel it was learned that nothing more had been seen of the small motor boat.

A log of the lifeboat shows clearly the extent of the search on that night. At 6.12 p.m. the engines were started and 3 minutes later she was passing the pierheads. At 6.30 p.m. St Martins Point was abeam to starboard and 35 minutes later the Queen Victoria was nearing the Hanois. The lighthouse was communicated with by both lamp and klaxon from 7.10 p.m. to 7.35 p.m. before there was a reply. An exhaustive search was then carried out in the vicinity of the Hanois. From 7.20 p.m. to 8 p.m. the Queen Victoria sailed WSW from the lighthouse and returned. She then proceeded for two and a half miles in a westerly direction. At 8.30 p.m. she was about a mile west on an opposite course and a half hour later was about one and a half miles off the coast south of Torteval Church. Orders were received by wireless telephone to close in to within a quarter to half mile of the Gouffre Hotel and subsequently at 9.30 p.m. the Queen Victoria was off Petit Bot and passed close to Les Lieuses rocks, which could be clearly seen. Coxswain Hobbs said that after about 8.30 p.m. visibility became poor. Continuing the search he closed into the Gouffre passing close to the Rousse and Le Balleine rocks.

At 10 p.m. when off St Martins Point, again the order was received by wireless telephone to proceed back to the Gouffre, stop engines and listen for megaphone calls. The motor boat 'Frolic' was eventually picked up between Icart and the Peastacks when Coxswain Hobbs sighted her on the sea side of the lifeboat about a mile to a mile and a half out. He thought at the time she might be making slight headway but there was a nasty lop running.

His offer to take the two fisherman aboard the lifeboat and put one of his own crew aboard the 'Frolic' was refused. However after refreshments had been taken the motor boat was taken in tow. The passage home was taken at a reduced speed as there was a big sea running in the freshening NE wind. The pierheads of St Peter Port were reached at 11.20 p.m. and five minutes later the Queen Victoria was along side.

The two men aboard the 'Frolic' were Mr William Bichard of Albany house, St Martins and Mr Herbert Sheppard of La Ramee. Once ashore, Mr Bichard explained the circumstances that led to their rescue. He said that they had left the Town Harbour shortly after eleven that morning in the 'Frolic' to lift crab-pots off the south coast. At around 5.30 p.m. they lifted the last pot near Torteval. Shortly after starting the motor it had failed and on closer examination it was clear that a petrol pipe had fractured.

He went on to say that owing to the high prevailing wind and sea they could make little headway. A little while later he observed the lifeboat pass on the outside and realised she must have been looking for them. Unfortunately neither man had any means at their disposal to signal the lifeboat but were eventually picked up and towed to the harbour.

The crew aboard the lifeboat were - Coxswain Fred Hobbs, 2nd Cox F Zabiela, A Gurney (Bowman), R Coles, W Hobbs, T Le Feuvre, B Noyon and A Stephens (Mechanic)

This was the second time during this year that Mr Bichard had been involved in a lifeboat rescue. On March 16th he had been aboard the fishing boat 'Leander' with Captain James Ingrouille when they had been towed to St Peter Port from a dangerous position off Fort Doyle. On that occasion they had been returning from an ormering trip to Herm.

Chapter 10

The Mayflower

On Wednesday 9th January 1935 the lifeboat Queen Victoria was summoned by maroons at 10.20 in the morning. Fifteen minutes later she proceeded through the pier heads under the charge of Coxswain Fred Hobbs with a full crew aboard. It had been reported by Captain Drummond Keane of the mailboat Isle of Sark which was at the time en route from Jersey to Guernsey that he had seen a small cargo steamer letting off a great deal of steam 3 miles south west of Sark.

The unknown steamer had hoisted two flags in signal but owing to the misty conditions it had been impossible to decipher the message. On seeing this Captain Drummond Keane immediately contacted Captain J Penstone Franklin the Guernsey Harbourmaster who saw fit to call out the Queen Victoria.

The lifeboat under the command of Coxswain Hobbs made course in a south-easterly direction which was witnessed by members of the lifeboat committee until the boat disappeared into the thick haze. Just after the Queen Victoria had left harbour a Mrs Carre of Plaisance, Sark contacted the Guernsey authorities to inform them that a steamer similar in appearance to the New Fawn was about three miles east of the Coupee. She said that the boat was still, with her bows pointing toward Sark but did not seem in difficulties.

Just after midday Mr W Frampton, Vice Chairman of the Lifeboat Committee reported that the Queen Victoria had located the vessel and that it was being taken under tow. It was found to be the Mayflower, a collier that had discharged her load at St Sampsons the previous day and had left that port at around 8.30 in the morning bound for Ronez in Jersey to collect a cargo of stone. Captain Atherton the skipper of the disabled ship said that they had left St Sampsons and had been under way for about half an hour when the boilers burst. At this point they were at the back of Sark and owing to the serious nature of the problem were unable to proceed. The 370 ton Mayflower owned by the Zillah Shipping Company of Liverpool was on its first trip to Guernsey and had left Britonferry on Saturday night with a cargo of anthracite coal for the island.

Coxswain Hobbs of the Queen Victoria stated that the steamer was sighted at about 11.10 about 4 miles east of L'Etac when the lifeboat was still some 5 miles away. However, owing to the favourable conditions they were able to make good headway and reached the Mayflower thirty-five minutes later. After ascertaining there were no injuries on board the lifeboat took the crippled steamer in tow when about 4 miles east of Sark Lighthouse. They set course for Guernsey via the north of Sark and the Lower Heads Buoy arriving back in St Peter Port at around 2.30.

The return of the two boats was witnessed by a large crowd that had gathered at the end of the White Rock. A small boy who had been watching the proceedings called out "Did your boilers burst" the only reply was a wry smile from Captain Atherton who was standing below the bridge of the disabled Mayflower.

In addition to Coxswain Hobbs the other members of the lifeboat crew were, F Zabiela (2nd Coxswain), A Gurney (Bowman), J Mauger, W Hobbs, C Farr, B Noyon and A Stephens (Mechanic). Second Cox Zabiela had boarded the Queen Victoria from the motor boat Celia off Herm.

Chapter 11

H.R.H Prince of wales

The islands most notable event of 1935 was without doubt the visit in July of H.R.H Prince of Wales. The Prince who was later to become King Edward Vlll arrived in Guernsey aboard the destroyer HMS Faulkner. It was originally planned that he would travel by seaplane and would be ferried ashore by the lifeboat. However his alternative mode of transport had made this option impractical. It had though always been intended that the Prince would board the Queen Victoria and meet the crew, he being the first member of the royal family to do so. The lifeboatmen were not disappointed when His Royal Highness arriving in a speedboat stepped on board the Queen Victoria before landing at No5 berth.

The cheers of the onlookers had subsided enough to allow the Prince to ask, "Who is the Captain?" At this point Coxswain Hobbs moved smartly forward and the Prince noted that he had a new boat. They spoke about the number of years the Queen Victoria had been in service in the island and the speeds she could achieve. The Guernsey Weekly Press of 27th July carries an excellent picture of the event with the heading "The Prince Afloat and Ashore – HRH on the lifeboat Queen Victoria having a happy informal chat with Coxswain Hobbs"

The Prince then turned to another member of the crew and enquired "When was your last service?" The reply came that it had been on 9th of January when the collier Mayflower was in trouble 4 miles east of Sark. The crewman then proudly added, "We saved the crew, ship and all" to which the Prince remarked "Good".

An unreported incident that occurred on this day has always been the cause of some amusement for members of the Hobbs family.

It is said that when the Prince stepped from the speedboat that he stumbled and was prevented from falling between the two boats by the strong arm of Coxswain Hobbs. The future Kings life had been saved!

HRH Prince of Wales aboard the Queen Victoria speaking with Coxswain Fred Hobbs

Chapter 12

The Lancashire

On the night of Tuesday 29th October 1935 a collier was sighted in distress on the north-east coast of the island. A strong west-north-west gale was blowing when it was decided that the Guernsey lifeboat should put to sea. The collier 'Lancashire' bound from St Peter Port had encountered a problem with her engines and was anchored near Houmet Paradis about two miles from Bordeaux. The first report of this impending disaster was made by P.C. Kimber who was on duty at the White Rock. He immediately informed the Harbourmaster that he had seen distress flares being put up in the vicinity of St Sampsons at around 7.20pm. Armed with this information the Harbourmaster called out the lifeboat.

The crew put in a prompt appearance and the Queen Victoria was under way by 7.45 under the charge of Coxswain Fred Hobbs. The firing of maroons had alerted the public and crowds quickly arrived at vantage points along the east coast to witness the progress of the lifeboat in the stormy sea. Early reports to shore from the Lancashire were not very clear to the cause or extent of the problem. They did however reveal that a crewmember had been slightly injured.

Further communications from the Lancashire by wireless and Morse lamps confirmed that her two anchors were holding and that she was not in immediate danger. At 9 o'clock a message was received from the Queen Victoria to say she was standing by. Meanwhile engineers aboard the Lancashire were attempting to make temporary repairs, and it was hoped that she would be able to make port under her own steam about midnight. However, due to the prevailing conditions the repairs took longer than first anticipated. This together with difficulties in pulling in her cables resulted in the Lancashire getting under way at around

12.15am. With the lifeboat in close attendance both vessels past Roustel Beacon en-route for St Peter Port at 12.20am. Ten minutes later the Queen Victoria radioed the message that the Lancashire had broken down again. Fortunately the crew of the Queen Victoria were able to get a rope onto her when only a ships length away from the rocks. Several people were watching at the Spur when the two vessels approached the pierheads at 1am.

The master of the Lancashire Captain A Smith of Cornwall stated later that during a heavy sea and strong wind a valve nut stripped causing the engines to break down. And while attempting to effect temporary repairs 2nd Engineer W Wilson was injured when a cylinder door fell on him. The Captain affirmed that his engineer had been lucky to escape with his life and was knocked out for several minutes. The lifeboat Coxswain F Hobbs told of the Queen Victoria's battle with the heavy seas. He said that the lifeboat stood by for three and a half-hours. The weather was terrible but temporary repairs to the engine were carried out. He went on to say that the ship had only moved about 3 lengths when she broke down again and the lifeboat had to take her in tow. When the Lancashire began to drift towards the rocks the lifeboats task became a difficult one and every ounce of power of the two engines had to be used to pull her clear just in time. Coxswain Hobbs paid tribute to both crews.

The 400-ton Lancashire owned by Messrs S B Ivan & Co had arrived at St Peter Port at 4 0'clock on Sunday afternoon from the north-east coast with a cargo of house coal for the Western Counties Association. After discharging she left in ballast at 6.30 on the Tuesday night and had been at sea less than an hour when the accident happened.

A letter in the Guernsey Weekly Press of 7th November from the Master of the crippled Lancashire paid tribute to the crew of the Queen Victoria. It stated "On behalf of myself and crew I wish to thank, through your paper, the coxswain and crew of the Guernsey lifeboat and everyone connected with the lifeboat for reaching us so quickly. The coxswain kept a watchful eye on us while we were disabled and it cheered my crew when the lifeboat told us they would stand by and render any possible assistance needed. The coxswain and crew had a hard time and deserve to be highly praised for their courage and cheerful messages sent to us in our time of need" He went on to personally thank the coxswain and lifeboatmen on behalf of all aboard the Lancashire. A letter in reply from Coxswain Hobbs praising the efforts and courage of the crew of the Lancashire appeared in the same newspaper. It stated the following. "The Coxswain and crew of the St Peter Port lifeboat wish to thank the Master and crew of the SS Lancashire for their letter of appreciation published in the Press. At the same time the lifeboat crew admires the pluck and perseverance of the Lancashire's personnel in working as they did under such difficult circumstances and imminent danger"

Chapter 13

The White Heather

The most unusual family reunion occurred on the night of 9th November 1935. The Brecqhou launch White Heather skippered by Fred Hobbs left Sark late in the afternoon bound for Guernsey. Aboard were a number of workers returning from Brecqhou for the weekend. Shortly after their departure the launch developed engine trouble and although the motor was re-started it failed soon after. Down to one engine and in the teeth of a strong southerly gale Coxswain Hobbs attempted to make for the shelter of Belvoir Bay in Herm but with a strong tide running this was found to be impractical. It was then decided that flares should be sent up even though the White Heather was in deep water and at that stage in no particular danger.

Back in Guernsey the lifeboat had been called out in response to flares that had been sighted 3 miles north of the Bec Du Nez in Sark. This first report at 7.05pm had come from a Mr Frost an employee of Captain Clarke in Brecqhou. A conflicting report had also been received from a police constable on duty at Bordeaux that he to had seen flares in the vicinity of the Platte Fougere. Although these reports did not coincide the lifeboat under the charge of 2nd Coxswain Fred Zabiela had no option but to steer a course northward up the Little Russel. Also aboard the lifeboat was crewman Bill Hobbs who was at that time totally unaware that his brother Fred's boat was in difficulty.

In gale force winds and a heavy squall the lifeboat steered a course up the Little Russel and when about a mile north of Roustel Beacon spotted a steamer showing lights and blowing her horn for a pilot. This had accounted for the flares seen from Guernsey. At about this time the Queen Victoria sighted flares across the Humps and subsequently had to navigate a precarious route between the small islets in face of the strong southerly winds.

At 8.25 a radio message from the lifeboat reported that flares had been seen to the east of Grand Amfrocque and that the lifeboat was at that time to the north of this point. Meanwhile relations of the passengers aboard the overdue White Heather were besieging the lifeboat station for news. Their patience was rewarded when at around 9pm news from the lifeboat reassured them that the White Heather had been located and taken under tow. Fred Hobbs had never been happier to see his brother and the valiant crew of the Queen Victoria. His report of events leading up to the rescue appear in the Guernsey Weekly Press of 14th November and are as follows.

The White Heather he said left Brecqhou at 3.55pm on Saturday afternoon and landed three Sark workmen who were returning for the weekend, at Saint de Juan near Harvre Gosselin. He left there at 4.10pm with seven persons on board including himself. This number including several Guernseymen who are employed on Brecqhou. When some little distance out said Mr Hobbs one of the engines became defective. The fault however, was located and remedied and the engine re-started successfully. About half an hour after that more trouble developed and the other engine stopped. In spite of all work on this engine it was found impossible to get going. Meanwhile with only one motor working, the White Heather was losing ground in the face of the southerly gale and the strong flood tide. The canvas was set and it was hoped to make for the shelter of Belvoir Bay. But at about 5.50pm the forestay-sail jib was blown away. With only one sail remaining and but a single engine this was found impossible and consequently the White Heather was kept in deep water for safety. He went on to say that "The White Heather was riding out the gale nicely she was shipping no water and making splendid weather. Although there was no danger out at sea I had to study the persons I had got on board. Consequently I gave orders for flares to be made and burnt, and was gratified to see the green star of the lifeboat maroon after the third flare. None of those on board were nervous, but I was perplexed when I saw the lifeboats

43

navigation lights and observed she was going down the small Russel. Meanwhile I kept the boats head to wind with the remaining engine running. Later the Queen Victoria came up and took us in tow, and we were able to assist with our one motor".

The lifeboat had found the White Heather at 9.10pm about six miles north-east of Herm and after taking her in tow steered a course down the Great Russel and through the Percee Passage arriving at St Peter Port at 10.30 in the evening

The crew of the lifeboat in addition to 2nd Coxswain Zabiela were Bowman W Gurney, lifeboatmen R Coles, W Hobbs, T Le Feuvre and C Farr. Motor Mechanic A Stephens and Assistant Motor Mechanic B Noyon.

Chapter 14

The Cloud of Iona

The first response to an SOS call by the Queen Victoria occurred on the evening of Friday 31st July 1936. At 8.15pm two rockets summoned the crew of the lifeboat to go in search of the Cloud of Iona a flying boat that was feared missing somewhere between Guernsey and Jersey.

After a swift turnout the Queen Victoria left the harbour mouth at 8.30 under the command of Coxswain F Hobbs.

The Cloud of Iona piloted by Captain W Halmshaw had reached Guernsey from Alderney just after 6pm and after unloading her passengers took on a further eight bound for Jersey. An hour later the plane made a perfect take off and disappeared into the gloom toward Jersey.

Alarm bells first rang when at 8pm Jersey Airways telephoned their Guernsey agents to report that the plane had not arrived. The lifeboat began her search in the direction of Jethou and the Ferriers and onwards to the western side of Sark. From there the Coxswain continued down the west coast of Sark through the Goulliot exploring the coast of Brecqhou on route. From here the Queen Victoria was headed southerly toward the Paternosters and Ecrehos off the Jersey coast. It was then the intention to search the west coast of Jersey in zig zag fashion across as far as the Minquiers but this plan of action had to be abandoned when orders from Guernsey re-directed the lifeboat back to Sark. Visibility was poor and nothing was sighted on the return crossing. The Queen Victoria resumed her search north of Sark until the early hours of Saturday morning. The order was then given to abandon the operation till half an hour before dawn at which point Coxswain Hobbs moored the lifeboat on Captain Clarkes mooring at Jacobs Head. The search continued at 4.30

the following morning sailing through the Goulliot Passage en route to Corbiere where it arrived at 6am. After making a further reconnaissance of Jersey's northern coast the lifeboat had to return to Guernsey for re-fuelling. The coxswain and crew came ashore for a well-earned rest and a substantial breakfast supplied by Stainers restaurant in the Pollet. Their search, in open sea had lasted 14 hours.

The second search began at 12.25 on Saturday afternoon when the Queen Victoria left St Peter Port bound for the French Coast under Coxswain Hobbs with crewmembers Zabiela, Gurney, Stephens and Noyon aboard. By 3.40pm the boat was 4 miles off Cape Carteret with still no sign of the missing seaplane. The order then came to set course for Guernsey and the lifeboat arrived back in the Town Harbour after a 24-hour search of which 21 hours were on the sea. As soon as he had landed Coxswain Hobbs telephoned home to tell them he had arrived, but, the future was still unknown. The Queen Victoria may still be needed. There was still no report of the missing plane.

Sometime later it transpired that the Cloud of Iona had hit a group of rocks close to Les Minquiers as personal effects and parts of the engines were found strewn on the reef. All eight passengers and crew were lost. Including a couple from Guernsey Mr E Appleby and Miss E Marley who were engaged to be married

The 'Cloud of Iona' on Braye Beach, Alderney

Chapter 15

The Spica

One of the most bizarre and almost unbelievable stories in the annals of local rescues must surely have occurred in the early hours of Thursday 22nd July 1937, when the motor yacht Spica drifted from the safe haven of St Peter Port harbour into turbulent seas off Brehon Tower. This was before her crew even realised that anything was amiss. The report in the Guernsey Weekly Press was headlined – Yachts Dramatic Drift While Passengers Sleep. The story that follows is an edited extract from that newspaper.

'The prompt action of a Police Officer and the Coxswain of the Guernsey Lifeboat averted in the early hours of Thursday what might have been a terrible tragedy. That the disaster was averted was due to the fact that at 12.30 that morning a yacht was sighted drifting in the harbour by Messrs Alfred & Harry De La Haye, States Houses, Bouet and Mr Creckley of No7 Allez St who were fishing. They informed PC Granger who was on duty at the White Rock. He rang Coxswain F Hobbs stating that a small yacht was drifting out of the harbour with her dinghy trailing astern. The police officer was surprised to see the boat drifting out and his amazement was increased when he hailed the yacht and received no response despite the fact that he was shouting through a megaphone. Coxswain Hobbs was at the pierheads within 10 minutes having summoned 2nd Cox F Zabiela to bring his motor boat Celia as the lifeboat was at that time undergoing a survey.

The story of the adventure was told us this morning by Coxswain Hobbs. He said that realising that with the wind west south west and a flood tide running the yacht would travel northward, he steered the Celia in that direction.

Aroused from Sleep

The drifting vessel was picked up between Brehon Tower and Platte Fougere. Mr Hobbs landed his brother on the yacht and as he did this the occupants of the yacht Spica owned by Mr JJ of 7 Canterbury Rd Oxford aroused from their sleep, came on deck. They had no idea they were adrift. The Spica, on which were Mr & Mrs Hunt and two gentlemen friends was brought back to harbour which was reached at 2.40am.

Rolling Heavy

Coxswain Hobbs said it was fortunate that these peoples plight was discovered, for sooner or later the yacht would have hit something. He went on to say that it was extraordinary that the occupants did not realise they were adrift because when discovered drifting towards a dangerous reef of rocks the yacht was rolling heavily.

It is believed the yacht was bumped by another boat and dragged her anchor. The Spica is a cutter of about 24 tons and Friday was lifeboat day! The 'press' boarded the Spica in the pool at 10.30 that morning and interviewed the owner. Mr Hunt smiled when he heard the object of the interview. "There is so little in it all" he observed. He then explained that they had entered St Peter Port harbour at 3.15 yesterday morning from Torquay. The Spica is a handsome 50ft cutter rigged yacht built in 1917 in Rotterdam. "I know these waters quite well and Guernsey too, we have been coming here for years" said Mr Hunt. "Yesterday we went ashore and had dinner ashore, we came back at about 10pm and went to bed". The Spica has 6 berths. "We certainly slept soundly, for it was only when the coxswain and party drew near that I heard men's voices, and of course I got up to investigate and then we all got up considerably surprised to find where we were". Mr Hunt paused then said, "It all arose because we didn't have enough chain out, and so we dragged the anchor". Mr Hunt and his party are staying here for a few days.'

It might appear that Mr Hunt and his party had probably wined and dined a little to well – perhaps a lesson to all seafarers.

Chapter 16

The Tommeliten

In 1938 the lifeboat was summoned a total of 6 times. The call outs during this year were varied and included a response to flares sighted off the west coast and the rescue of three boys in a rowing boat near Herm.

The first service rendered was on Wednesday 12th January after a report was received from Cherbourg stating that a French aircraft had ditched into the sea somewhere between Guernsey and Jersey. An air and sea search began immediately to discover the whereabouts of the mystery plane. In response to this request for assistance the Queen Victoria put to sea to search the waters between the two islands. When interviewed on his arrival in Jersey Coxswain Hobbs said the lifeboat had made a search of the southwest coast of Guernsey and then made a zigzag course in the direction of Jersey, nothing was seen except for a barrel of Briesis wine. There was a report of a French seaplane in the area that was in difficulties but it was thought that it had sorted its problems and no wreckage had been found during the search.

Three weeks later at the end of January the Queen Victoria was in action again as a result of a dramatic call for the lifeboat in response to an SOS from a French army plane which was reported down off Guernsey. The Queen Victoria was called at 3.30 pm and at 3.40 pm went out of the harbour at fine speed. A later message stated that the French plane had come down with engine trouble but that another French plane had noticed her plight and landed nearby. It was later understood that the plane was down four miles south west of the Hanois. The lifeboat with Coxswain Hobbs, Lifeboatmen H Hobbs, W Gurney and A Stevens aboard reported that they were three and a half miles south west of St Martins point and had seen no signs of a plane.

The lifeboat was recalled later in the evening on confirmation of the message from Brest that the crew of the aircraft were safe.

On the 6th March the lifeboat turned out to attend the SS Tommeliten which had struck a rock in dense fog while attempting to enter St Sampsons harbour. Aware of the imminent danger the Captain took the wise decision to beach his ship near Bordeaux.

The Queen Victoria put out from St Peter Port at 10 o'clock with a full crew under Coxswain Hobbs and immediately made her way to the scene of the wreck. Coxswain Hobbs said later when interviewed that the lifeboat arrived off Bordeaux but it soon became obvious her assistance was not needed. The Tommeliten was by then high and dry and a number of small boats were around her. The Queen Victoria returned to St Peter Port where hundreds had gathered to witness her return. Stiffness in her steering gear was rectified before she was returned to her moorings. The Tommeliten was bound for Guernsey with a cargo of coal and was approaching St Sampsons where she anchored. On resuming she struck a rock and finally Captain Williams had to beach her. She was of 288 tons and carried 500 tons of anthracite coal, coming from Port Talbot in Wales. She was refloated the same evening and slowly made her way into the safety of St Sampsons harbour.

On Tuesday 17th May Mr G Douglas of St Martins had an exciting adventure in his yacht White Wings in Belle Greve bay. Just after 5pm Mr Douglas left St Sampsons with the intention of sailing to St Peter Port. A gust of wind caused the yacht to heel over flooding the cockpit. There was no help at hand and Mr Douglas clambered onto the side of the hull to await help, hoping because of his position he had been spotted. The news of the accident reached Coxswain Hobbs and he boarded a boat belonging to Mr Carre of Northside and set out at all speed with Mr Carre on board. On arrival the White Wings was taken in tow to St Sampsons where she was pumped out by Mr Douglas who then returned home none the worse for wear.

On the 29th of July, a situation that could have had serious consequences fortunately ended happily when three boys were rescued from a rowing boat near Herm. The boys, two brothers and a cousin, Norman, Arthur and Douglas Banton had set off in a small boat with the intention of going to Herm. When approaching Brehon they realised the tide was too strong. They turned the boat and made for Guernsey only to find the tide was even stronger. They eventually managed to secure themselves and the boat to a post and tried to signal the mailboat Sambur to no avail. Then at about 10.45pm night-watchman G Mahy on duty at St Sampsons noticed the flashing of a yellow light in the Little Russel. He contacted the Harbourmaster Captain Frankland who had already been informed by the captain of the Sambur that three boys had been spotted in difficulty near a beacon close to Brehon. Within three minutes the rockets had been set off and within another ten the lifeboat Queen Victoria was under way under the command of Coxswain Hobbs. At around 11.38pm a report from the lifeboat stated that a small boat with three boys on board had been spotted close to Corbette de la Mare beacon and that they were about to be taken aboard the Queen Victoria. A call was put back to the lifeboat to confirm the identities. Once known the parents of the boys were joyous to hear that their sons were safe. By this time a large crowd had gathered at St Peter Port. They had not long to wait for within 20 minutes Coxswain Hobbs was bringing the Queen Victoria alongside the Cambridge Berth. Onlookers could see through the hatchway of the main cabin three faces and a large tin of biscuits and it was obvious that the three boys were safe and uninjured.

A letter of thanks appeared in the 'Press' the following week from Mr A W Banton thanking all involved for the safe return of his two sons and nephew.

In September the lifeboat was called out after distress flares were reported off the west coast. Shortly after 10pm on Tuesday 27th the lifeboat slid quietly through the pierheads under Coxswain Hobbs with a full crew. At 11.25 the Queen Victoria passed west of the Hanois but nothing was to be seen. The night was clear and visibility good. The lifeboat continued up the west coast some 8 to 10 miles out and circumnavigated the island, returning to her moorings at 2.15am.

When interviewed, Coxswain Hobbs told how he received his notification at home at 9.50pm. Fifteen minutes later with a full crew aboard and after one of the quickest turn outs the Queen Victoria passed the pierheads. Making a southerly direction towards Le Gouffre they established contact with a steamer that had reported Verey lights, as had the keepers at Les Hanois. The coxswain concluded by emphasising that conditions were ideal. The sea was calm and visibility perfect. He went on to add that they could see for miles around and there was nothing whatever from which to conclude that a vessel might be in distress.

Chapter 17

The Occupation Years

One of the most heartrending decisions facing Guernsey families in the early months of 1940 was whether to stay put, or evacuate to England. As time went by the signals became clearer and suggested that the island would suffer the same inevitable invasion already experienced in France. Some felt it wiser to remain and take their chances, others were keen to move their young children away from a hostile advancing enemy as soon as possible.

In Alderney however the situation was slightly different, perhaps because of its proximity to France or the overwhelming fear of isolation felt by the population as a whole. On Saturday 22nd June, Judge French, the President of the States of Alderney addressed a meeting of islanders on the Buttes to ascertain the general feeling among the thousand strong crowd. He told them that the Germans were coming and that they were in danger of their lives. He added that he had applied to the British Government for evacuation shipping and that they should decide as a whole whether to go or stay. After a short pause he heard shouts of "Let's go"

The following morning six ships arrived at dawn and embarked around eleven hundred people. After an uneventful crossing the flotilla docked at Weymouth late on the Sunday evening. On his arrival Judge French immediately sent a telegram to the Guernsey Bailiff – Ambrose Sherwill stating that Alderney had been evacuated, apart from nineteen people who had refused to leave. Being aware that the northern isle would be an easy target for German invasion, Mr Sherwill ordered Fred Hobbs to take the lifeboat to Alderney on the Monday morning to bring the remaining persons back to Guernsey, by force if necessary. After this most difficult assignment Grandpa reported the following.

"Arrived at 10am and left about 10.30am. The pilots, Jack Quinain and his two sons were then preparing to leave at midday. There was a French fishing boat in the harbour. The instructions before we left Guernsey were to release all cattle etc. We had stretcher cases but owing to the weather we put back into Alderney and left about 3pm arriving at Guernsey at about 6pm. I had to see Mr Batiste who asked us to bring down some documents. As we came through the town together, Mr Batiste pointed out one shop that had been broken open, I think it was Bucktrouts, I saw no sign of any other premises having been broken open."

A hand written note in the Guernsey Archives indicates that the lifeboat brought some of the remaining islanders, but not all back to Guernsey. The following day Mr Sherwill sent over a force of fifty-two men, some armed, to encourage those still there to leave. Even they were not totally successful in bringing all off the island.

Back in Guernsey people were still unsure of the future, some had already gone others had yet to make up their minds. In the case of the Hobbs family the split was almost half-and-half. Grandpa and Grandma stayed, as did their children Harold, Alec, Pat and my mother Merlin. The remainder including Ruth, Dolly and Olive had gone to England whilst the younger two Joan and Win had been evacuated with their respective schools. As coxswain of the lifeboat, it may have been a sense of duty that kept Grandpa in Guernsey, that we might never know. But the decision was to have dire consequences.

On the afternoon of Friday 28th June, he received orders from R.N.L.I. headquarters to muster two crews. His mission was to proceed immediately to Jersey to collect their lifeboat Howard D and return both boats to England, thus preventing them falling into enemy hands. With the Queen Victoria at Cowes for overhaul, Fred Hobbs and his crew aboard the relief boat Alfred and Clara Heath left St Peter Port harbour at 4.05pm bound for Jersey. Those on board included his two sons Harold and Alec, 2nd Cox Fred Zabiela and his son Fred, Gerald Dunstan, the

English mechanic who had come over with the relief boat, and local bowman Bill Gurney. Harold had not wanted to go on the trip but was encouraged to do so by his father who knew there were no crewmembers in Jersey available to make the crossing.

It was a fine afternoon when the Alfred and Clara Heath passed the pierheads en–route for Jersey. The journey went well until about 6.45pm when the boat was almost abreast of Noirmont Point. At that moment a crewmember noticed clouds of smoke rising into the evening sky over St Helier. Second Cox Zabiela jokingly remarked that "The Germans had landed in Jersey" no sooner had his last word been uttered, when a group of three planes approached from the stern, diving down on them with machine guns blazing. The crew was in total disarray and just couldn't believe what was happening to them. Grandpa quickly took avoiding action by steering a zigzag course and told the crew to take cover. Unfortunately the design of the relief boat afforded little protection and after an attack lasting nearly twenty minutes the planes moved off in another direction. Several shots had hit the boat, one of these killing Harold outright. The mechanic Gerald Dunstan having escaped with a minor graze to his knee. Following this assault Fred made for Elizabeth Castle where he moored temporarily. Finding that they needed to move into the harbour proper before being able to get ashore the engines were restarted, no sooner had the engines sprung back into life when more planes returned, this time dropping bombs. Fortunately for all concerned the enemy had missed their target on this second occasion. After some minor engine trouble and when the skies became a little clearer the Alfred and Clara Heath was berthed at St Helier where the crew put ashore. They were accommodated at the Aurora Hotel and the Jersey authorities telephoned the R.N.L.I. to inform them of the tragedy. It was decided at this point that the Howard D should remain in Jersey. Grandpa had also by this time telephoned home to pass on the sad news of Harold's death. After the inquest Grandpa stated that he wished to convey his son's body back to Guernsey but on Monday July 1st the Germans occupied Jersey and the plan to bring Harold's body home had to be forcibly postponed.

Following their arrival in Guernsey the previous day the German Harbourmaster had set up headquarters in the Ship & Crown Hotel. My mother who was only sixteen at the time and grief stricken at the news of her brothers death, forced her way into his office demanding to know when her father and brothers were returning to Guernsey. The officer, obviously embarrassed by what had taken place was extremely sympathetic and said that the attack on the lifeboat should never have happened. He informed my mother that the pilots were only supposed to be on a reconnaissance mission and had since been severely dealt with. This though was very cold comfort and my mother and grandmother kept vigil at the harbour each morning hoping to see the boat returning from Jersey, until finally on Wednesday July 3rd the boat was sighted. The German authorities had wanted Harold to be buried in Jersey but Grandpa insisted that he should return home aboard the lifeboat with his crewmates. After 3 days, permission was finally granted and the Alfred and Clara Heath with two German guards aboard and aircraft overhead came into St Peter Port carrying Harold's coffin draped with a Union Jack. The simultaneous attack that had taken place in Guernsey claimed the lives of 34 people on that day. Their names along with Harold's are remembered on a memorial plaque sited the top walk of the White Rock pier.

The 33 year old Harold left behind a 3 year old son Tony and grieving widow Betty.

Harold Hobbs with his wife Betty near the Town Church

There has since been a great deal of criticism of this raid, the fact that the Channel Islands had been declared open ports and that the British Government had failed to properly inform the Germans has been seen as a major blunder. However, in Ralph Durands book Guernsey Under German Rule published in 1946 he fiercely condemns the way in which the enemy had such little regard for human life. In particular he mentions the attack on the Guernsey ambulance which clearly displayed a red cross. But he was even more outraged by the assault on the lifeboat which was in open sea and could not have been mistaken for any other type of craft. This is what he said.

"It might even be possible – should anyone care to make the effort – to exonerate the shooting of people in the Grange and on the deck of the 'Courier'. There is however one incident of the raid which the most earnest German apologist will find impossible to justify, excuse, or even palliate. Life-boats should be regarded by belligerents as especially immune from attack because it is their noble duty to serve, not the people of any individual country, but humanity as a whole. Yet one of the

planes fired on the Guernsey life-boat, killing one of her crew. No sophistry, however ingenious, can excuse that outrage. The machine gunner cannot have hit the life-boat by accident when aiming at something else, for the life-boat was well out to sea and no other target was within range. He cannot have mistaken the lifeboat for any kind of small naval auxiliary vessel for the boats of the Royal National Lifeboat Institution differ so conspicuously in colour and design from any other kind of craft that it is impossible to mistake them. The machine gunner who fired on the life-boat must therefore have known well what he was doing and his act must be classed with those acts of "schrecklichkeit" (frightfulness), approved by German war lords when they feel strong enough to defy the international laws that regulate civilised warfare, and perpetrated for the purpose of terrifying civilian populations. In fact the cold blooded murder of the life-boat man suggests that the main purpose of the raid was to strike such terror into the hearts of the people of Guernsey as would ensure their docility when the time came to occupy the island."

"At the going down of the sun, and in the morning,
we will remember them"

Queen Victoria dressed overall

Following the arrival of the German forces life on Guernsey changed dramatically for its people. The rules and regulations laid down were very strict and meant that the remaining population would have to adhere to a way of life that they had never before experienced.

The deprivations they encountered took many different forms. However the situation in the Channel Islands was somewhat different to that of the already occupied European countries. The islands being British were classed by the Nazi regime as being a special case, one which could be viewed as a template for a future invasion of mainland Britain. With complete control of all aspects of daily life the Germans were able to manipulate the local authorities, islanders and workforce to best suit their needs. Men were told that providing that they were not directly involved in assisting the occupiers in a military capacity then this satisfied the rules as stipulated by the Hague convention. However the Germans found ways to circumvent these rules and many islanders complied, sometimes under the duress of not knowing the outcome should they refuse. Lorry drivers delivered materials and labourers worked on projects that today would probably challenge the spirit of the convention.

With his marine experience my grandfather was seconded by the Germans to act as pilot, being one of the few still on the island with the ability to safely move large ships in and out of St Peter Port harbour. His skill in this area was well respected and he was called upon regularly to perform these tasks. As a result he established a civilised working relationship with Capt. Obermeyer the then acting Harbourmaster. Sometimes challenging, over time the men developed a mutual respect for each other. Obermeyer had been the master of ocean going liners prior to the war and understood the hazards the role of a pilot could sometimes entail.

Captain Obermeyer

Grandpa was ordered on many occasions to take parties of officers and troops to the Hanois, Casquets and other islands. My mother related that there were many instances when soldiers had begged him to take them to England but his fear for the safety of his remaining family was utmost in his mind and he absolutely refused to do it.

During the early years of the occupation his job was to act a skipper of the White Heather for its owner Captain Clarke of Brecqhou. This boat made daily trips to Sark to supply its inhabitants and provide a vital link between the islands. The record shows that many medical cases were also carried to and fro. As food and other commodities became shorter the advantages of these daily trips became evident, Sark being more relaxed and less controlled by its occupiers, fish, butter, vegetables and even clothing were occasionally available if you knew the right people. There follows an extract from my Mothers memoirs which bears this out.

"My fathers trips over to Sark were sometimes quite fruitful, he would bring back a quarter pound packet of tea which was then kept for special occasions, in the meantime we had to drink 'tea' made from dried bramble leaves. Sometimes he might bring a bag of flour or a packet of salt which was worth its weight in gold. How the Sarkees managed to hide all this stuff away from prying German eyes was remarkable. Once he brought me back a length of navy blue material and told me to make it up into an afternoon dress, instead of which my sister Pat produced a panelled skating dress, very smart but he was furious. Another time he managed to obtain a pair of green suede boots but they were a half size too small, however I squeezed my feet into them probably ruining my toes for life."

The boat also made frequent trips to Alderney, Herm and Jethou transporting agricultural machinery, produce and cattle at the behest of the Controlling Committee and under the watchful eye of the Germans.

Whilst growing up my mother had often said to me that she had helped her father to write up his logs and how unfortunate it was that they had been lost. Each night on his return she had transcribed the handwritten notes from his on-board journal into the formal ships logs. These showed a daily record of the movements of the White Heather together with crew lists, cargo and any other relevant information pertaining to the boats operation.

Some years after my mothers passing I was fortunate to receive two of these logs that covered the years 1942-43. They were passed to me by a cousin living in England who had been given them by her mother for safekeeping. Both documents bore out my mothers accurate description of the professional way in which her father approached his work. The meticulously entered details relate to the day to day workings of the boat. As with any information of this sort some entries are fairly standard but there are some that could be regarded as being of historical interest. In particular the recording of movement of German shipping. This could have been viewed as sensitive at the time, it was however likely that the Germans if they were aware of it overlooked this potential breach of security. The other information he was careful to include were the names of Sark people leaving and returning to the island and in particular those who had been selected for deportation.

The logs have since been micro filmed and are available for public viewing at the Priaulx Library, however there follows a selection of some of the more interesting entries.

Friday May 1st 1942
No sailing for White Heather this day.

Monday May 11th 1942
No sailing for White Heather this day. Hobbs proceed to Sark with German boat H.S.16 returned back from Sark at 6pm. 20 passengers

Thursday July 2nd 1942
White Heather left Guernsey for Sark at 10.10am with cargo for German troops and Sark. Returning leaving Sark for Guernsey at 5pm, arriving at 6.15pm with German horse and cargo for troops. Feldkommandant and staff from Grange Lodge on board. Received 10 gallons of petrol. 40 Passengers.

Monday Sept 21st 1942
No sailing for the White Heather this day.

The evacuation of British people from Guernsey started today.
522 British mols?

Ship Robert Muller No8 and Steamer La France

Saturday Sept 26th 1942
White Heather left Guernsey for Brecqhou and Sark at 10.05am with passengers, mail and cargo. After landing food at Brecqhou proceed to Sark, arrived at noon. White Heather left Sark for Guernsey at 4pm with British evacuation people from Sark. Mr & Mrs Moore, Mr & Mrs Beaumont, Mr & Mrs Thomason, Mr Jenkins and 3 children. Arrived at Guernsey at 5.25pm. Strong NE wind and rain. Mr & Mrs Skilton? missing.

26 Passengers.

Sunday Sept 27th 1942
No sailing for the White Heather this day.

Mrs Skilton brought over to Guernsey by Sark Protocol boat.

540 Evacuees left Guernsey at midnight.

Sunday Oct 4th 1942
No sailing for the White Heather this day.

At 6am called out for Sark which was postponed at 9am. Proceed with Tug D.19 to escort ship in distress on the Oyster Rocks south of Castle Cornet. At 11.15am Escort ship re-floated undamaged and brought into St Peter Port harbour with motor boat Myca with Capt. Obermeyer on board. Proceed on to Brecqhou around and back to Guernsey at 6pm with Capt. Obermeyer on board.

Tuesday Oct 6th 1942

At 10am White Heather all ready for sailing to Sark. Weather too bad, fog all day. St Peter Port closed to all shipping and no sailing to Sark this day. All work finished at 5pm.

Mr J Carre, Fisherman of Sark was arrested by the German Police in Sark and taken to Guernsey

Saturday Oct 10th 1942

White Heather left Guernsey for Sark at 10.15am.with cargo and 12 passengers and mail.

Mr J Carre, Sark fisherman crossed to Sark after being released from the German Police.

White Heather left Sark at 2.25pm for Brecqhou to land food, after landing same proceed on to Guernsey with 7 passengers and mail. Arrived Guernsey at 4.30pm. Strong SW wind. 19 Passengers

Friday Oct 16th 1942

No sailing for White Heather this day. Loading cargo for Sark.

At 2.15pm left Guernsey for Sark with MY Moya with Capt Obermeyer and Officers on board. Proceeded to Dixcart Bay and returning back to Sark Harbour landed Capt. Obermeyer to invoice all Sark fishermen with new orders to fishing. The motor yacht Moya left Sark again at 7.45pm for Guernsey with Capt. Obermeyer and all officers on board. Arrived at 8.45pm

Monday Oct 19th 1942

At 1.30am Received telephone message to stand by to pilot motor yacht Seewatch to Sark with General and Staff.

At 7am left Guernsey for Sark with Seewatch, left Sark again at noon with the General and 8 Officers.

No sailing for White Heather this day. 9 Passengers

Friday Oct 23rd 1942
White Heather left Guernsey for Herm at 10am with Guernsey farmers Mr E J De Garis in charge of party at Herm and 3 Germans. Landed Mr De Garis at Jethou

Mr and Mrs Dickson left Herm to live in Guernsey. White Heather left Herm at 7.15pm for Guernsey with Mr De Garis and party of farming men, 10 sheep and 2 heifers.
Arrived at Guernsey at 8pm. 15 Passengers

Arrangements are being made by Mr De Garis and Captain Franklin Harbour Master for the transferring of all Mr McDonalds furniture from Jethou to Herm by the MV White Heather.

Mr De Garis was landed at Jethou by Captain Hobbs and son at 11.30am to make arrangements with Mr and Mrs Mc Donald for the evacuation of Jethou

Mr and Mrs Dickson was removed from Herm to Guernsey by orders of the German Authorities, Grange Lodge. Mr and Mrs Dickson crossed over to Guernsey by the White Heather and all baggage. – 10 Passengers

Thursday Oct 29th 1942
White Heather all ready for sailing to Sark and Brecqhou at 10am but it was decided by Capt Hobbs the weather was too bad, strong ENE wind and rain and the White Heather remained in St Peter Port harbour

The first evacuation took place April 3rd 1941

Loyans and De Boue returned back to Brecqhou on the 18 of April 1942 and left again on October Friday 30 1942

Friday Nov 20th 1942
No sailing for the White Heather this day

At 1pm FC Hobbs left Guernsey for Sark with the German Pilot Boat Le Cerf with Capt Obermeyer, the General and Mr Peterson on board. At 4.30pm the German Motor Pilot Boat left Sark for Guernsey.

Arrived in St Peter Port at 5.30pm and landed all the party.

Saturday Nov 21st 1942
The White Heather left Guernsey for Sark at 10.15am with cargo, 34 passengers and mail. After landing all passengers, mail and cargo in small boats the White Heather left Sark for Guernsey at 3.05pm with 22 Sark evacuees to live in Guernsey and furniture brought to Guernsey by White Heather and 68 Germans troops (the word troops crossed out). – 129 Passengers in all to and from Sark

Friday Dec 18th 1942
The White Heather left Guernsey for Herm at 10.30am with the Guernsey farming party and one load of hay. Jurat E De Garis in charge of farming party. JA Bourgaize, JN Dorey, AD Le Patourel, H Ogier, RG Dorey, JA De Garis, RG Froome, F Browning, NJ Brouard, HO Le Patourel. Landed party at 11.10am. The White Heather left Herm again at 3.15pm with 13 head of cattle for Guernsey and the party of 11 farmers. Arrived at 4pm with cattle at London Berth. At 6pm piloted Steamer Schokland into St Peter Port at No5 New Jetty. NW wind and rain – 11 Passengers

Thursday Dec 24th 1942

The White Heather sailing was postponed owing to sharp shooting by the German forces from 9.30 till 1pm. The White Heather was all ready to leave Guernsey at 1pm, this sailing was also postponed till 9am Friday.

- 1943 -

Friday Feb 12th 1943

No sailing for White Heather this day. Crew working on White Heather loading coal and oil. Capt Franklin loan Mr Charles Perry at Sark 20 sacks for coal (12/2/43) Weather strong NW wind rain at times.

25 Sark people left Guernsey at 6.30pm for Germany and 135 Guernsey people by the steamer La France. Seen off by the Bailiff Victor G Carey and Mr HE Marquand States Supervisor, John Leale, RH Johns, RO Falla, Capt E Cowley and the Acting Inspector Lamy of Police.

10.45am the German Steam Tug O19S left Guernsey for Sark with 20 passengers mail and cargo. Arrived in Sark at noon and landed all passengers and cargo. At 2pm the German Steam Tug O19S left Sark for Guernsey with 25 Sark people internees for Germany, the names are

Mr & Mrs E Baker not left Guernsey

Mr & Mrs P Carre not left Guernsey

Mrs Campbell, Miss Cheeswright, Rev & Mrs Phillips, Mr & Mrs Wallroth, Mrs McDill, Mrs Buchan, Mr & Mrs E Falle and Miss G Falle not left Guernsey. Miss Quigley, Miss Watts, Miss Carter, Mrs Gallienne, Miss Gallienne & Master Gallienne, Mrs Mollet, Misses B&E Bouget, Mr H Carre La Collinette, Mrs Pittard, Mr & Mrs P Carre La Collinette not left Guernsey. Misses E Page & Miss Duckett, Mr RW Hathaway, Col. EJE Fear, Mr & Mrs G Sharp. Mr J De Carteret not left Guernsey.

List of persons evacuated from Sark on Friday February 12th 1943.

Nurse Le Tissier and Mr Le Tissier left Sark for Guernsey. Mrs Le Tissier for hospital.

FC Hobbs was Pilot of the steamer O19S this day.

Left Guernsey at 6.30pm by steamer La France – 40 Passengers

My grandfather continued to run the White Heather between Guernsey and Sark up until February 15th 1944 at which time he suffered a serious head injury as a result of an accident which rendered him unable to carry out his work and eventually leading to his death. On that day he was collected by some German sailors in a car at ten in the morning with a view to visiting Fort Doyle, it was reported that at some stage they had visited a canteen at Les Vauxbelets where he had allegedly fallen down some stone steps and hit his head.

The White Heather under German guard in Creux Harbour Sark

After the incident he was delivered back home at which time Doctor Gibson was called. He diagnosed that he was suffering concussion and needed to be treated in hospital. However he had previously told his friend Lacey Hamon that they had been to Jerbourg and Les Hanois and had been involved in a motor accident. The suspicious circumstances of his death have always been called into question by the family bearing in mind that the German authorities would at that time have been quick to distance themselves from any suggestion of foul play. The accident that eventually led to his death was witnessed only by some German sailors and it has to be observed that a prominent gold ring that he wore together with some gold sovereigns that he kept in his money belt were never recovered. He died a month later on 13th March 1944. The following report appeared in the Guernsey Press on 15th March 1944

Death of Lifeboat Coxswain –GEP 15th March 1944

The death is announced of Mr C.F. Hobbs, for many years the coxswain of the lifeboat Queen Victoria. Mr Hobbs, who resided at Armada Place, St Clement Rd, was 60 years of age and died at the Emergency Hospital on Monday after a months illness. He was for some time employed by Capt. T.A. Clarke of Brecqhou and until just previous was in charge of the White Heather on the Sark service.

Evidence at Inquest

An inquest was held this morning before Jurat Quertier Le Pelley, Coroner, into the circumstances surrounding Mr Hobbs death. Mrs Reta Hobbs declared that on Tuesday, February 15th, her husband left home with some work-mates at about 10 a.m. to go to Fort Doyle. When they returned at 2 p.m. his companions dragged him from the car and put him in the sitting room. When asked what had happened, they said Hobbs had fallen down two metres of steps. His hand was bruised and his clothing dirty. Next morning he had not recovered consciousness, so Dr. R. E. Gibson was called in, and he ordered Mr Hobbs removal to the Emergency Hospital. He was brought home again and seemed to improve a little, but after consultation with another doctor, was once more removed to the hospital.

Mr Alec Royston Hobbs (son) stated that when he saw his father, he formed the conclusion that although he had had some drink, there was something else wrong. Despite enquiries, Hobbs never said anything of what happened.

Mr Lacey James Hamon said that Hobbs told him he had been to Jerbourg, the Hanois, and back to Jerbourg on the day in question, and they had a smash with the car, and he did not like it.

Dr R.E. Gibson deposed that when called to Hobbs' house, he thought he was suffering from concussion of the brain. He was sent to hospital, but was allowed to go home later, when he became troublesome. As the doctors were not satisfied as to the cause of death, a post-mortem examination was carried out. It revealed a fracture of the skull, laceration and haemorrhage, which caused death. The inquest was adjourned for one week, pending further enquiries.

The inquest of Coxswain F.C. Hobbs was continued this morning.(16th March 1944)
A report from the German authorities concerning his death was read to the court by Police Inspector A.P. Lamy. It was stated that Hobbs fell down some steps at the Vauxbelets; he was not drunk at the time. Nothing was known of a motor accident, and the statement of the deceased about such must be attributed to the head injuries received. "There was no evidence of foul play" said the coroner, returning a verdict of Death by Misadventure.

INQUEST ON COXSWAIN HOBBS - GEP 27th March 1944

Second Inquest into the death of F.C. Hobbs 27th March 1944

The magistrate today continued the inquest started on 15th March 1944 for Frederick Charles Hobbs aged 60 who died on 13th March 1944 in the Emergency Hospital, Castel. The magistrate examined a report written by Officer Von Pach of the German Feldgendarmerie. At the close of the enquiry on 15th March it stated that the said Hobbs had left home around 10 a.m. accompanied by German sailors in a car with the intention to visit the German canteen at Les Vauxbelets in St Andrews. He had probably fallen down a flight of stone steps, had lost consciousness and was taken home. On the 17th February he was taken to hospital where he died on 13th March of lacerations to the brain and a fractured skull. The injuries he received were due to the said fall but there was no proof of how the said Hobbs had fallen down the stairs.

These inquests are available for viewing at the Greffe, Guernsey.

The Funeral

A large crowd gathered for the funeral at Le Foulon on 16th March including the crew of the lifeboat, family, States members and a German contingent headed by Captain Obermeyer and Dr Graeff. After the committal prayers Captain Obermeyer speaking in English gave a short oration before placing a wreath bearing the inscription 'Der Hafenkommandant, Guernsey'. He concluded his speech by paying tribute to the professional way in which my grandfather had carried out his work.

Although being a senior member of the occupying forces Captain Obermeyer was well respected by the local population especially the fisherman who benefitted greatly in many ways due to his generosity and fairness.

In fact there were many Guernsey people who visited him in Hamburg after the war. He and his wife were by that time suffering the deprivations of a broken country where food and essential commodities were in very short supply.

However, life for the Obermeyers was made a little more bearable due to the kindness shown by some islanders who provided the couple with much needed food parcels. They had not forgotten his assistance and understanding during a time of great strife.

So here concludes the story of my grandfather Frederick Charles Hobbs. A man that I never knew but a man of whom I am immensely proud.

Printed in Great Britain
by Amazon

12103486R00047